Betty,

May your
journey through life
be blessed with
hope, faith and joy.

Carolyn

Voyages

written and designed by
terri hoyland

Voyages

a collection of quotes and affirmations
so when we occasionally grow weary on
our journey through life, we can stop and
renew our wellsprings with feelings of
peace,
    joy,
        hope,
            love.

written and designed by
terri hoyland

First printing, May 1993
by Terri Hoyland

Printed in the United States of America

ISBN 1-883794-20-X

Printed by Pepco Litho, Inc., Cedar Rapids, Iowa
Published by Heartlights Imagery, Inc.
P.O. Box 36
Cedar Rapids, Iowa 52402

This book is dedicated to
Nancy Bayliss *who opened
my eyes to a new level of spirituality...
and* **Wayne Bayliss** *who constantly
challenges me about how to apply
this spirituality to all aspects of
the real world.*

Dear Friend,

These pages were deliberately left untouched to remind us all of our many imperfections and humanness.

We hope you look beyond the mere words to seek their true meaning and see your own reflection. The hand written texts remain in that form so that you may identify with them just as if you had written them yourself.

Any references to "man" in quotes remains as originally written by the author. Our interpretation of what it means to us is expanded beyond the literal interpretation of the meaning of the word "man" to include <u>all</u> men and women.

Peace be with you on your journey,
Heartlights Imagery

P. O. Box 36
Cedar Rapids, Iowa 52406
(319) 366-2041

I understand

I understand the seasons.
the Glory.
the Death
the Resurrection
the Peace
I understand winter's rest
to appreciate the soul for spring's celebration...
daffodils' power to push through frozen soil.

I understand purple.
I understand the labor of planting...
the visualization of the harvest.

The summer heat invites gnats to suck on my neck,
as sweat leaks from my temple,
I understand the heat and the gentle breeze that teases me.

I hear growth.
I understand green
I understand the autumn...
fullness touching the harvest.

I understand the death of leaves.
Orange all around me demanding to be seen
and then flutter to their maker, the soil.

The earth gets ready for bed.
I understand winter's white.
the Night
the Angels
the Peace

                                    Dianne Brown Ross

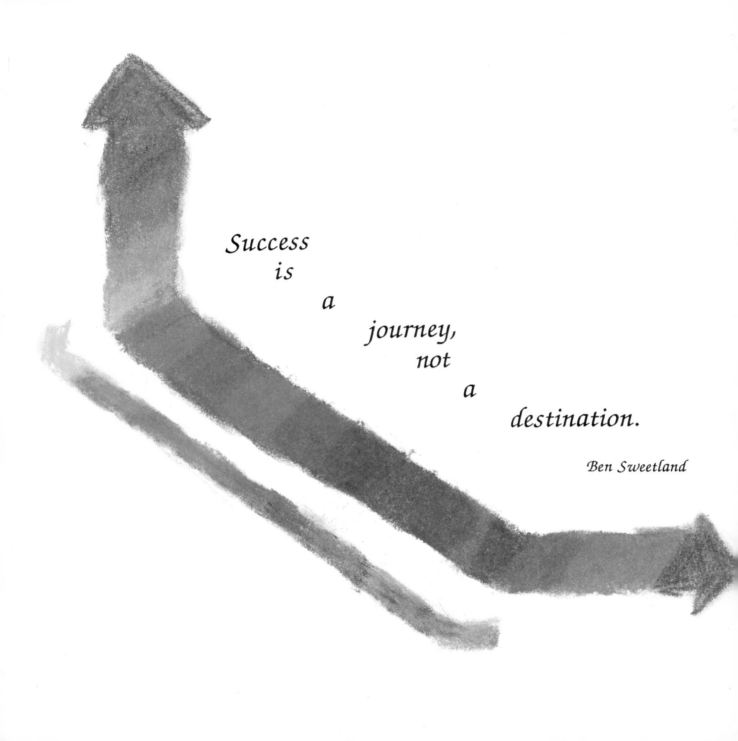

Success
is
a
journey,
not
a
destination.

Ben Sweetland

I've begun a journey through life
to fulfill my potential.
I have so much to learn.
This journey takes me through many
twists and turns.

I will be successful
even when I face adversity
or challenges or fear.

I am determined to overcome every obstacle
on my path.

I look forward to my journey,
to see what there is to see,
learn what there is to learn,
do what there is to do,
love what there is to love.

I CHOOSE TO MAKE MY LIFE SUCCESSFUL.

When you pray
go into
your inner room.

Matthew 6:6

On my journey through life
Sometimes I need to rest and reflect.
With each breath I take
I grow calmer and more peaceful.

I breathe in gentleness and
    breathe out rigidity.
I breathe in awareness and
    breathe out confusion.
I breathe in courage and
    breathe out fear.
I breathe in openness and
    breathe out the need to be judgemental.
I breathe in the ability to trust and
    breathe out rejection.
I breathe in hope and
    breathe out despair.
I breathe in strength and
    breathe out failure.
I breathe in love and
    breathe out anger and hate.

In the calmness of my heart
I find wisdom and serenity.

*You cannot discover
new oceans
unless you have
the courage to lose
sight of the shore.*

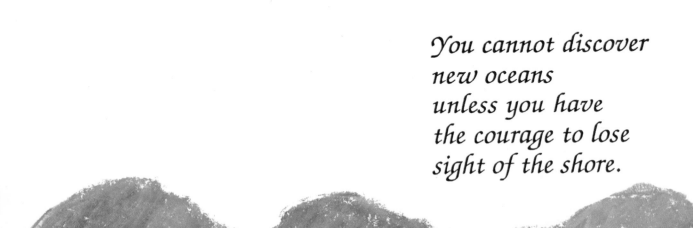

It takes courage to give up
something we know is safe and secure
when I'm not sure what lays ahead.

Yet if I don't, I may never know or feel
  - the exhiliaration of new unfelt highs
  - the satisfaction of achieving a goal
  - the strength of overcoming obstacles
  - the joy of learning
  - the peace of understanding.

I gather together all my strength, my dreams,
    my hopes, my vision,
    and set off on this wonderful new journey.

Where it takes me, doesn't matter.
    It only matters that I learn about myself
    and overcome my fears.

I AM OPEN TO NEW EXPERIENCES.

Do not follow
where the path may lead...

Go instead
where there is no path
and leave a trail.

I have no desire to go through
life just getting by.

I want to live each day to its fullest.

In order to do that,

I follow my own path.
I listen to my own conscience.
I do what feels right for me.

I call upon my inner resources of:

wisdom
courage
hope
joy
love.

I AM IN CHARGE OF MY OWN LIFE.
OTHERS MAY FOLLOW ME.

*You can do
what you have to do,
and sometimes you can do it
even better
than you think you can.*

Jimmy Carter

Those words "I can't..."
ring in my head when I face something difficult.

I take a deep breath.
I take another and feel calmness flow over me.
I say to myself:
    I know I have the courage to overcome fear.
            I've overcome others.
    I have the wisdom to plan to proceed ahead.
    I have the patience to be good to myself while
        I work through this.

I smile to myself and know...

   I CAN!

"*Do not fear the winds of adversity. Remember a kite rises against the wind rather than with it.*"

Hamilton Mable

when the winds of adversity
knock at my doorstep,
I open and embrace this challenge.
I choose to see this as an adventure,
an adventure to move me into
new direction.

I choose to leave behind feelings of failure,
of not measuring up,
that it is someone else's fault.

I am ready to move on.
I look inside and ask myself
what can I learn from what happened?
What steps can I take to grow from this?
How can I turn this from a negative
into a positive situation?

I rise to the challenge knowing:
I am capable,
wise,
open,
learning.
I AM STRONG ENOUGH TO OVERCOME.

Face it.

Face it, and it'll vanish.

Evan Hunter b. 1926

I feel such fear, hurt, anger, disappointment.
and I want to run from it,
but I don't.

I turn and face it.
I step into it.

I feel the pain fighting within me.
I wonder if this pain will ever stop
when I begin to feel throughout my body:
I am worth loving.
I am wonderful!
I am special.
I am doing my best.
I am courageous.
I am filled with goodness and beauty.

I feel myself growing stronger
and the pain is beginning to subside.
I feel calmer.
I breathe in more strength.
I realize I am alone and at peace.

I HAVE LET GO.

"*Every man I meet
is in some way my superior.
In that way I learn from him.*"

Ralph Waldo Emerson

Every time I am with you,
I have an opportunity to learn and grow.

whether you are
                rich or poor
                        strong of body,
                        weak of mind,
                                man,
                                        woman
                                                in charge or
                                                        hired hand,
                I see your own value.

You may teach me to see life in its simplicity.
You may show me how to appreciate others around me
You may exemplify the value of hard work.
You may understand temptation and how to overcome it
You certainly bring a different perspective.

                Thank you for being you.

                I see your beauty.

                When I learn from you,
                I learn about me.

"Bless your enemies.
They enable you to grow."

Buddhist belief

No one said life would always be easy.

There are some people in my life with whom
I will not get along.

Let me look at this as an opportunity,
    an opportunity to grow.

        Opportunities include:
            to forge a better understanding of our differences,
            to see myself through their eyes,
            to stand in my truth when necessary,
                knowing I am principled and honorable,
            to accept differences as part of life,
            to love myself and others unconditionally,
            to learn to forgive and let go of
                grievances, real and imagined.

As I learn these hard lessons,
        my heart is lighter,
            my mind is clearer,
                my body is energized,
                    my spirit is freer,
                        my soul is pure.

He that cannot forgive
others
breaks the bridge
over which
he must pass himself;
for every man
has need to be
forgiven.

Lord Herbert

I wish I didn't make so many mistakes,
but I make mistakes every day,
and some of those mistakes have hurt others.

I regret words I've said, things I did.
I slip up just when I think I've licked it.

Yet I know I really want to be better.
I try hard but know I must
accept my humanness, my imperfections.

I forgive myself for being thoughtless or hurtful.

In so doing, I remind myself
that each person does the best they can...
that they are also confined by their humanness.

Let me not judge lest I be judged.

I forgive you knowing I will seek
forgiveness along the way.

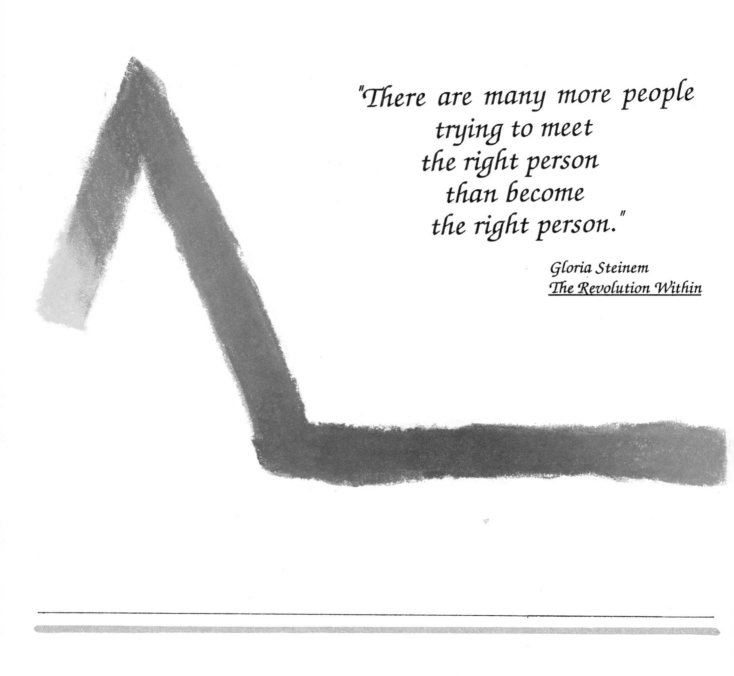

"There are many more people
trying to meet
the right person
than become
the right person."

Gloria Steinem
The Revolution Within

Sometimes it seems easier to think
  the world around me reflects my worth:
      marrying the right person,
      following the right career path,
      holding the right credentials,
      befriending the right people,
      living in the right neighborhood,

It may even give me a false sense of importance.
    Yet no other person reflects who I really am.
When I am alone, I look into myself.
I look into my heart to see my real reflection:

sensitive,	loyal	honest
caring	fair.	understanding
loving	tender	strong

I know what I truly want to be more of:

loving	non judgemental
honest	open
patient	creative.

    I like the person I am and am becoming.

    LET THE REAL ME SHINE THROUGH.

"The best
and most beautiful things
in the world
cannot be seen
or even touched.
They
must be felt
with the heart."

Helen Keller

My heart feels:

joy   forgiveness
love   wonder
hope   trust
peace   freedom
awe   strength
curiosity   acceptance
wisdom   tenderness
excited   empathy
connected   understanding

They are in abundant supply
    when I open my heart.
I want to receive these gifts.

I CHOOSE TO FEEL BEAUTIFUL THINGS.

"Treat a man as he is,
and he will remain as he is;
treat a man as he can and should be,
and he will become as he can and should be."

Goethe

I care about you.
I want you to be your best
  so I won't support your limitations, your weaknesses.
      Accept them, yes.
      Understand them, yes.
      Support them, no.

I want you to stand on your own two feet,
  feel your strength,
  own your beauty and integrity.

I know you are capable of
  being greater than you are right now.

    I BELIEVE IN YOU.

"You can't have trust without being trustworthy."

Anonymous

I believe I am a special person.
  I am capable of making hard decisions.
  I am strong enough to carry them out.
  I am aware of the feelings of others.
  I am honest and hard working.
  I am flexible and able to change.
  I admit my mistakes.
  I learn from my experiences.

Therefore I trust myself.
I behave in ways that are trustworthy
It reflects my trustworthiness.
Regardless of what anyone else says or does
I look in the mirror
and know I am trustworthy.

I have high expectations for myself.

I live up to these expectations.

MY BELIEFS AND ACTIONS MATCH.

...*when you're feeling helpless and hopeless,*
the worst thing you can do is just stand back
and let people rescue you.

Linda Henley b. 1951

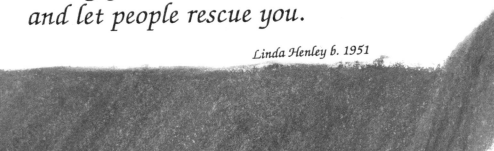

There are times when I feel
overwhelmed, discouraged or lost.

I know you want to help me.
    Let me hear your optimism.
    Let me rest upon you.
    Let me have your advice.

        But don't do it for me, for it is my life and my choice.

I must take charge so I learn I can do things for myself.

        I am strong.
        I am intelligent.
        I am capable.
        I am decisive.

If you do them for me, you tell me I'm not those things.
        The truth is . . .
            I AM.

"The ability to feel is indivisible.
Repress awareness of any one feeling
and all feelings are dulled.

The same nerve endings are required for
weeping and dancing,
fear and ecstasy."

Fire in The Belly
Sam Kean

Sometimes I want to shut out
feelings of loss, anger and betrayal.
I want to lock them behind my mind's
door as if they didn't exist.

When I do so, I also cut off my
feelings of joy, hope, awe and begin to feel...
                    nothing.

Let me look at them anew...
        My anger teaches me to give up control
            for I have none over anyone or
            anything other than myself.
    When I feel betrayed,
        I learn to take care of myself
        and see my own uniqueness.
    When I lose someone I love,
        I learn to appreciate the moment
        and live it fully.

My fear teaches me to listen to my own wisdom
and follow my own advise.
I accept these feelings as part of my journey through life.
I move through them and find...

        I AM AT PEACE.

The finite mind
does not
require us to
grasp the infinitude of truth,
but only to
go forward
from light to light.

Peter Bayne

There are so many things that happen that
I simply do not understand.
I ask why do we lose ones we love,
    why is there suffering,
    why do bad things happen to quality people...
I don't know why.

I believe there is some sort of master plan
way beyond my human comprehension.

What I do know is that
    experiencing love is the utmost joy,
    even as losing love is the deepest pain.
If I have to choose between
    feeling love or not feeling it,
    I'll choose to experience love.
I am especially blessed when
    you give me your gift of love in return.
    It shines forever in my heart even after you go.
Then, two lights of love shine - yours and mine.

I go forward sharing my heart with another...
    and another...
        and another.
    LET MY LIGHT SHINE.

We may change
with the seasons
but the seasons
will not change us.

Unknown

I open my eyes to new life in springtime;
 I choose to feel hopeful.

I delight in the fruitfulness of summer;
 I choose to feel joy.

I reap the harvest of life's experience in the fall;
 I choose to sing their praises.

I rest in the solitude of winter;
 I choose to feel at peace.

I enjoy the changing seasons for they bring opportunities.
 I CHOOSE MY OWN WAY.

"... the final forming of a person's character
lies in their own hands."

Ann Frank

I know I am truly responsible
for what happens to me.

I can't blame my parents,
my spouse or my job.

I am in charge.
    I accept this willingly.
I make my own choices.
    I seek a quality life.

        Whether I allow life to pass me by
        or I make things happen,
        it is up to me.

I decide how I look at life.
    I embrace it willingly.

Who I am and who I become
        is up to me.

"There is plenty out there for everybody. This abundance mentality flows out of a deep sense of personal worth and security. ...It recognizes unlimited possibilities for positive interactions, growth and development."

Stephen R. Covey
Principle-Centered Leadership

I believe I am a special person.
I know I have a lot to give to this world.
I know I'm not the only one who is special.
You are too.
I recognize that and sing your praises.
I give you credit for what you've achieved.
I rejoice in your good fortune.
     Your success doesn't mean less success for me.
     In fact, I can learn from you.
     I am inspired anew.

When we work together, our combined talents
     bring a new expanded potential,
          create a different way of seeing,
               complement our differences.
     We move toward balance and harmony.

     You and I share a new way of being
     where each reaps abundantly.

I HONOR THE YOU, THE ME AND THE WE.
TOGETHER OR APART, THERE IS PLENTY.

Life is like a path
and we all have to walk the path.
If we lay down,
we can lay down on that path.
If we live through the night,
we have to get up and
start walking down that path again.

As we walk down that path,
we'll find experiences
like little scraps of paper
in front of us along the way.

We must pick up those scrap pieces
and put them in our packets...

Then one day, we will have enough
scraps of paper to put together
and see what they say.
Maybe we'll have enough to make some sense...

Read...
then put the pieces back in that packet
and go on,
because there will be more pieces to pick up...

Uncle Frank Davis
Pawnee

I have so much to experience
        as I go through life...

            I will enjoy,
                leavn,
                    grow,
                        love each day,

        I believe each situation, activity,
        like each piece of a puzzle,
        adds to the whole
                and when life is over
                it is complete...

                and understood.

To order *Heartlights* products:

	Price	Quantity	Total
Heartlights			
Reflections of the love within your heart			
Garden Sojourn			
Guided journey tape	$ 9.98		
Musical journey tape	$ 9.98		
Book of quotes & affirmations	$14.00		
Voyages			
Learning to expand beyond our limitations			
Finding courage and imagination to take			
control of our lives			
Guided journey tape	$ 9.98		
Musical journey tape	$ 9.98		
Book of quotes & affirmations	$14.00		
Connections			
Feel oneness with nature and God			
Understand our relationship with others			
Guided journey tape	$ 9.98		
Musical journey tape	$ 9.98		
Book of quotes & affirmations	$14.00		

Send order to:

Heartlights Imagery, Inc.

P. O. Box 36
Cedar Rapids, Iowa 52406
(319) 366-2041

	Total
Sub-total	
Tax (Iowa only - 5%)	
Shipping & handling	$ 4.00
TOTAL	

SHIP TO:
Name _____
Address _____
_____
Phone ( ) _____

PAYMENT METHOD:
____ check ____ Mastercard ____ Visa
_ _ _ _ _ _ _ _ _ _ _ _ _ _ _ _ Exp _____